MOVE AND GET HEALTHY!

EAT A RAINBOW
HEALTHY FOODS

WRITTEN BY
SUSAN TEMPLE KESSELRING

ILLUSTRATED BY
TATEVIK AVAKYAN

magic wagon

Content Consultant:
Pamela Van Zyl York,
MPH, PhD, RD, LN

VISIT US AT WWW.ABDOPUBLISHING.COM

Published by Magic Wagon, a division of the ABDO Group, PO Box 398166, Minneapolis, MN 55439. Copyright © 2012 by Abdo Consulting Group, Inc. International copyrights reserved in all countries. All rights reserved. No part of this book may be reproduced in any form without written permission from the publisher.

Looking Glass Library™ is a trademark and logo of Magic Wagon.

Printed in the United States of America, North Mankato, Minnesota.
102011
012012

 THIS BOOK CONTAINS AT LEAST 10% RECYCLED MATERIALS.

Text by Susan Temple Kesselring
Illustrations by Tatevik Avakyan
Edited by Melissa York
Series design and cover production by Emily Love
Interior production by Craig Hinton

Library of Congress Cataloging-in-Publication Data

Kesselring, Susan.
  Eat a rainbow : healthy foods / by Susan Temple Kesselring ; illustrated by Tatevik Avakyan ; content consultant, Pamela Van Zyl York.
     p. cm. — (Move and get healthy!)
  Includes index.
  ISBN 978-1-61641-858-8
  1. Nutrition—Juvenile literature. 2. Fruit—Color—Juvenile literature. 3. Vegetables—Color—Juvenile literature. I. Avakyan, Tatevik, 1983-, ill. II. Van Zyl York, Pamela. III. Title.
  RA784.K3994 2012
  613.2—dc23
                                        2011033080

TABLE OF CONTENTS

EAT HEALTHFUL FOOD

You need healthful food to grow, play, and learn. Healthful foods have nutrients. Nutrients help you grow strong. Some nutrients are proteins, fats, carbohydrates, vitamins, and minerals.

Eat many different foods every day. This helps you get all the nutrients you need. Then you stay healthy.

ENERGY FOR YOUR BODY

Proteins, fats, and carbohydrates give your body energy. We count this energy with calories. Fats have more calories than proteins or carbohydrates.

PROTEIN FOR STRONG MUSCLES

Protein is part of all living things. It is part of all the cells in your body. Protein helps you grow. It makes your muscles stronger. Protein helps your body fight sickness, too.

FOODS WITH PROTEIN

Meat, fish, eggs, dairy foods, and nuts all have protein. Beans such as black beans and baked beans have protein, too.

Eat foods that have protein with every meal.
You can drink milk or eat peanut butter on toast at
breakfast. Enjoy a bean burrito or a ham sandwich
for lunch. You can eat baked chicken or a veggie
burger at dinner. Have some almonds as a snack.

GOOD FAT

Your body needs good fat to
stay healthy. Healthier fats come
from plant foods. Less healthful
fats come from some types of
meat and animal foods. You do
not need to eat very much fat.

GRAINS FOR ENERGY

Eating foods made from grains gives you energy. Grains are the seeds of some plants. Grains have carbohydrates. Carbohydrates are fuel for your body.

Grains have vitamins and minerals. Grains have fiber, too. Fiber helps your stomach work well. It helps you feel full longer. Your body can't digest fiber. It passes through your body instead.

There are two types of grain foods: whole and refined. Whole grain foods use all the parts of a grain. Whole wheat bread, brown rice, and oatmeal are some whole grain foods. Whole grain foods make you feel full longer.

A whole grain can be split. This makes a refined grain. Refined grains use only part of a grain. White bread and white flour are made from refined grains. Refined grains are less healthful than whole grains.

13

Where can you find grains? The bread in your sandwich is made from grain. Your breakfast cereal is, too. Pasta and tortillas are made from grain. Rice and corn are also grains.

Eat foods made from grains at every meal. Eat more foods made from whole grains than refined grains.

HEALTHFUL SNACKS

A healthful snack has protein and carbohydrates. Eat whole grain crackers with peanut butter or almond butter. Try hummus in a whole grain pita. You will have tons of energy! Add tasty veggies for crunch and vitamins and minerals.

FRUITS AND VEGETABLES

Fruits and vegetables are grown around the world. And there are many ways to enjoy them! You can cook them. You can eat them raw, frozen, dried, or canned. Or, you can drink them as juice.

Fruits and veggies have vitamins and minerals. They are full of fiber. They help you stay healthy.

NOTHING ADDED

The most healthful fruits and vegetables have nothing added. Ask grown-ups for 100 percent juice. Ask for canned or frozen fruits and veggies with no added salt or sugar.

Veggies and fruits come in many colors. Different colors have different nutrients. So, eat a rainbow of fruits and veggies! Eat dark green spinach and bright orange carrots. Eat blue blueberries, red strawberries, and golden peaches.

Make half your plate veggies and fruits at each meal. Eat berries at breakfast. Munch on carrots or an apple at lunch. Add sliced peppers to your snack. Eat salad or broccoli at dinner. Have pears or melon for dessert. They are naturally sweet!

VITAMIN FOODS

Carrots have vitamin A. Vitamin A keeps your eyes healthy. Strawberries have vitamin C. Your body needs vitamin C to heal scrapes and cuts.

DAIRY FOR STRONG BONES AND TEETH

Dairy foods are made from milk. They give your body calcium. Calcium is a mineral. It makes bones and teeth strong. Eat dairy foods three times a day. This gives you the calcium you need.

LIKE A ROCK

Your body needs iron and calcium. These are minerals. Minerals are in many foods. But they are also found in rocks! Most rocks are made of several minerals.

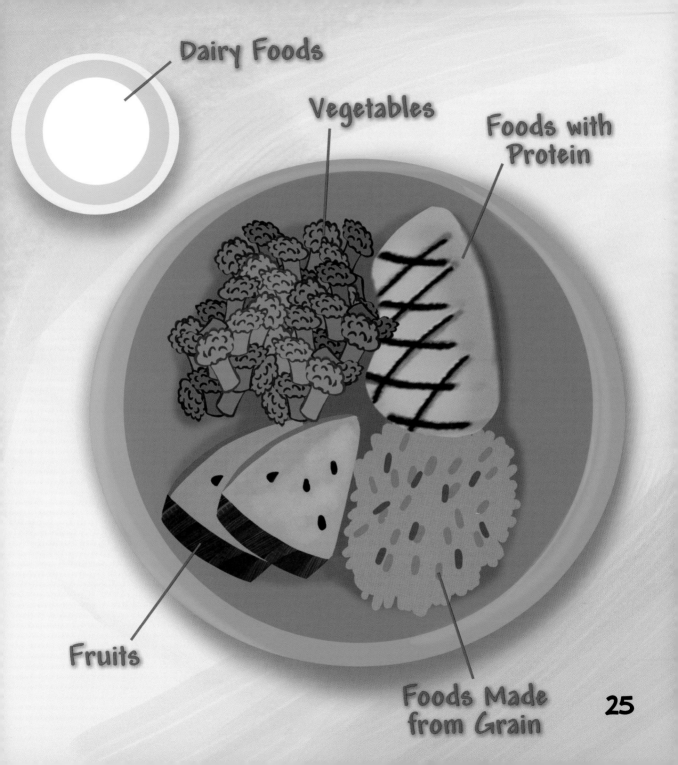

Dairy Foods

Vegetables

Foods with Protein

Fruits

Foods Made from Grain

25

WHAT ABOUT OTHER FOODS?

Foods like cookies, candy, and potato chips are "sometimes foods." You should only eat them sometimes. They give you energy, but the energy goes away fast. They do not have many vitamins and minerals.

Soda is mostly sugar. Drinking water or milk is much better for you. Sip water when you feel thirsty. Drink more water if it is hot or if you are playing hard.

27

EAT A RAINBOW

Healthful eating is easy and tasty! Use MyPlate to remind you what to eat at every meal. Drink lots of water. And remember to eat a rainbow. Eat many kinds and colors of food. They will keep you growing, healthy, and strong—and full of energy!

29

GET HEALTHY

1. Try a new fruit or vegetable. Try pomegranate in the winter. Inside this fruit's peel are tiny round seeds that you eat. Try kohlrabi in the summer. This vegetable looks like a green head with tall leaves for its hat. Ask a grown-up to peel it and cut it up for you. It's crunchy and juicy like an apple.

2. Make your own yogurt parfait. First, find a see-through glass or dish. It needs to be a little taller than it is wide. Put some plain yogurt in the bottom. Then add a layer of your favorite fruit. Add another layer of yogurt. Add one more layer of fruit. If you want, you can put some granola or another favorite cereal on top. Your yogurt parfait looks pretty and tastes great!

3. Feeling hungry after school? Make your own pizza! Take half of an English muffin. Whole wheat is best. Spread some tomato sauce on it. Cover with shredded mozzarella cheese. Add green pepper, olives, tomatoes, broccoli, mushrooms, red or yellow peppers, onions, or whatever you like. With a grown-up, put your pizza in a microwave oven. Heat your pizza until the cheese is melted and bubbly.

4. For a different kind of frozen treat, try a banana pop! Cut a banana in half. Peel half of it. Put a popsicle stick into the cut end. Spread peanut butter on the banana. Roll it in crispy rice cereal, granola, or chopped nuts. Put it in the freezer until frozen.

WORDS TO KNOW

calories—units of measurement for energy, especially energy from food.

carbohydrate—a nutrient that gives your body fuel.

digest—to break down food.

energy—being able to do things without feeling tired.

mineral—a substance found in rocks, the ground, and the food you eat. Some minerals are nutrients your body needs.

muscle—body tissue, or layers of cells, that help the body move.

nutrients—the parts of food your body needs to live and grow.

protein—a nutrient your body needs to build cells and to grow.

refined—with some parts taken out.

vitamin—a nutrient your body needs that is found in different types of food.

LEARN MORE

BOOKS

Chancellor, Deborah. *Healthy Eating*. New York: Crabtree Publishing Company, 2009.

Miller, Edward. *The Monster Health Book: A Guide to Eating Healthy, Being Active and Feeling Great for Monsters & Kids*. New York: Holiday House, 2008.

Rockwell, Lizzy. *Good Enough to Eat: A Kid's Guide to Food and Nutrition*. New York: HarperCollins, 2009.

WEB SITES

To learn more about healthy foods, visit ABDO Group online at **www.abdopublishing.com**. Web sites about healthy foods are featured on our Book Links page. These links are routinely monitored and updated to provide the most current information available.

INDEX